iPhone 15
Seniors Guide

Your Simple Path to Mastery and Connection: Easy Steps, Large Illustrations, Big Text, and Handy Tips for Non-Tech-Savvy Users.

TechBoost Publications

Table of Content

Dear Reader,

We are truly proud that you have chosen us as your guide into the fantastic world of iPhones. This book is our first publication, crafted with love and dedication. At TechBoost Publications, we bring together software developers, IT consultants, and trainers with extensive experience in the digital world, united by the desire to create useful content for both those new to electronic devices and software, as well as for experts and professionals. In the coming months, we have plans for new books dedicated to artificial intelligence, software, and new digital tools that, if used correctly, can enhance our daily lives, boost creativity, and become valuable allies in our business and careers.

Our experience as trainers has taught us that even those without a technical background can learn to use technology effectively, provided they have the right words and tools. We hope this book serves that purpose for you.

If you find our project helpful and feel inclined to support us, simply leave a review on Amazon. It may seem like a small gesture, but it means the world to us: it shows that our effort and care in publishing this volume have been appreciated by those who matter most to us: our readers. We don't want you to feel obligated, but we want to let you know there's a way to encourage us to continue with this project: just scan the QR code in the square below. How do you do that? Open your iPhone's Camera app, point it at the QR code, and tap the notification that contains the link. You'll be redirected to the Amazon page where you can leave a review for the book.

Before you continue reading, we want to let you know that as a token of our appreciation for choosing us, we have included QR codes on the last few pages that will grant you access to some bonus content with further insights and tips that we hope you will enjoy.

Happy reading!

Introduction

In an era defined by rapid technological advancements, understanding and harnessing the power of modern devices is essential for staying connected and improving our quality of life. Innovations such as smart homes, wearable technology, and advanced mobile devices are transforming everyday experiences, making it crucial to familiarize ourselves with these tools. Amidst these innovations, one device stands out for its blend of sophistication and accessibility: the iPhone 15.

This device exemplifies how technology can seamlessly integrate into our lives, making daily tasks easier and more enjoyable. It's not just a phone; it's a versatile tool designed to enhance every aspect of modern living. With a sleek design and user-friendly interface, it caters to both tech-savvy individuals and those who are less familiar with digital gadgets. Navigating the digital age becomes significantly more manageable with the right tools. This iPhone offers an intuitive interface that prioritizes ease of use, making it accessible for everyone, including older adults who might find modern technology daunting. By simplifying complex tasks, it ensures that users can stay updated and connected without feeling overwhelmed. Embracing modern technology also means opening up to new ways of connecting with the world. iPhone 15 facilitates seamless communication, allowing users to effortlessly keep in touch with family and friends. Whether through video calls or instant messaging, staying connected has never been easier, helping to bridge distances and strengthen relationships.

Moreover, the device's potential to improve daily life extends beyond communication. It integrates features that cater to health, security, and personal interests, making it a comprehensive tool for modern living. As we delve into its functionalities, it becomes clear that this iPhone is designed to be more than just a smartphone. It's an all-encompassing device that supports various aspects of life, from health monitoring to staying organized and entertained.

Understanding how to use this technology effectively is key to unlocking its full potential. This guide aims to demystify iPhone 15, providing clear and straightforward instructions to help users navigate its many features. By doing so, it empowers users to take full advantage of what the device has to offer, making life easier and more fulfilling.

At TechBoost Publications, we understand that adopting modern technology can be daunting, especially for seniors who might not have grown up with digital devices. Our mission is to bridge the gap between advanced technology and those who find it intimidating, ensuring that everyone can benefit from the digital age. The iPhone 15, with its thoughtful design and user-friendly features, is a prime example of how technology can be made accessible and empowering. This guide is crafted specifically for seniors, providing clear, step-by-step instructions to help you navigate the device with confidence. We start with the basics, breaking down complex tasks into simple actions. From setting up your device to understanding its core functions, our goal is to make the learning process smooth and enjoyable, transforming the iPhone from a source of frustration into a valuable tool.

One of the standout features of this guide is its focus on accessibility. The new Apple device is equipped with a robust suite of tools designed to cater to diverse needs. Features like VoiceOver, which provides spoken descriptions of on-screen elements, and the Magnifier, which turns the camera into a digital magnifying glass, are invaluable for those with visual impairments. We offer detailed instructions on how to activate and customize these features, ensuring that you can tailor your device to your specific needs.

Staying connected with loved ones is a top priority for many seniors, and the iPhone 15 excels in this area. Whether through FaceTime video calls or Messages, this device makes communication seamless and enjoyable. Our guide walks you through the setup and use of these features, offering practical tips to enhance your experience. From adjusting volume settings for clearer audio to using the built-in camera to capture and share special moments, we ensure that you can make the most of your device's capabilities.

Health and safety are also critical concerns that the iPhone 15 addresses effectively. The Health app tracks vital metrics and wellness information, offering a comprehensive view of your health. The emergency SOS feature ensures quick access to help, offering peace of mind whether you are at home or on the go. We provide clear, step-by-step instructions to help you use these features confidently, ensuring that your health and safety are always supported

Embracing modern technology is not just about keeping up with the times; it is about enriching your life and staying connected with the world around you. With the iPhone 15 and the comprehensive support of TechBoost Publications, you have the tools to navigate the digital age confidently and enhance your daily experiences. Let us guide you on this journey, helping you unlock the full potential of your device and embrace the many possibilities it offers.

Chapter 1

Introduction to Your iPhone 15

Unboxing Your iPhone 15

Unboxing a new device, especially something as advanced as the iPhone 15, can be an exciting experience. The sleek packaging of the iPhone 15 is designed to give you a glimpse of the elegance and sophistication of the device inside. When you open the box, the first thing you will see is the iPhone itself, beautifully encased in a protective film to ensure it arrives in perfect condition. Lift the device out to reveal the accessories neatly tucked beneath it. You will find a USB-C to USB-C cable for charging and data transfer, which is essential for setting up and using your iPhone. If you have your own charging brick, you can use it, but if not, consider purchasing an Apple or compatible third-party charger for best performance.

Next, you'll notice the small booklet that includes the quick start guide, warranty information, and two Apple stickers. The quick start guide provides a brief overview of the essential features of your new iPhone, making it a handy reference as you begin to explore your device. For users in the United States, it's important to note that the iPhone 15 supports eSIM only, meaning there is no physical SIM card slot. This digital SIM provides cellular connectivity and can be activated through your carrier without the need for a physical SIM card.

With your iPhone 15 and accessories laid out, it's time to start setting up your device. Begin by pressing and holding the power button on the right side of the iPhone until the Apple logo appears. This signifies that your device is powering up. You'll be greeted with a "Hello" screen in multiple languages. Swipe up from the bottom of the screen to start the setup process. You'll be prompted to select your preferred language and region, which will customize your iPhone's settings accordingly.

Next, you'll connect to a Wi-Fi network. This step is crucial as it allows your iPhone to activate and connect to Apple's servers. Choose your Wi-Fi network from the list and enter the password to connect. Once connected, you'll proceed to the Data & Privacy screen, which provides information about how Apple uses your data. Tap "Continue" to move forward.

The next step involves setting up Face ID, Apple's facial recognition feature that allows you to unlock your phone securely and authorize purchases with a glance. Follow the on-screen instructions to scan your face. If you prefer not to use Face ID, you can opt for a passcode instead. It's advisable to set up both for added security.

After setting up Face ID or your passcode, you'll have the option to restore data from an existing backup or set up your iPhone as a new device. If you're upgrading from an older iPhone, you can transfer your apps, data, and settings seamlessly using

Quick Start, which involves placing your new iPhone near your old one and following the on-screen instructions. For eSIM activation, you'll need to follow your carrier's instructions to transfer or set up your cellular service digitally.

As you complete the setup, you'll reach the Home screen, the central hub of your iPhone 15. Here, you'll see familiar apps like Phone, Messages, Safari, and Photos, as well as new additions that come with the latest iOS update. Take a moment to familiarize yourself with the layout. The bottom row, known as the Dock, holds your most frequently used apps for easy access. You can customize the Dock and Home screen by rearranging apps and creating folders.

Well done, you have successfully unboxed and configured your iPhone 15! Now, you're ready to explore its features and capabilities, making the most of your new device. Remember, this is just the beginning of your journey with your device. Each step you take will bring you closer to mastering this powerful tool and staying connected with your loved ones and the world.

Understanding the Interface

Learning the layout of your iPhone 15's interface is key to becoming comfortable with your new device. The home screen is your starting point, where you'll find a grid of app icons, each representing a different function or application.

One of the standout features of the iPhone 15 is the new Dynamic Island, which replaces the traditional notch at the top of the screen. The Dynamic Island is a versatile area that adapts to show important notifications, ongoing activities, and shortcuts to apps in use. For example, if you're on a call, playing music, or using a timer, you'll see live updates in the Dynamic Island, allowing you to multitask efficiently.

Navigating your iPhone involves using various touch gestures. These gestures might feel unfamiliar at first, but they will become second nature with a little practice. Here are some key gestures to get you started:

Swipe Up from the Bottom: This brings you to the home screen or allows you to switch between recent apps. If you're in an app, swiping up and pausing in the middle of the screen will show all open apps, making it easy to switch between them.

Swipe Down from the Top Right Corner: This opens the Control Center, where you can quickly adjust settings like brightness, volume, Wi-Fi, and more. Don't worry if this feels a bit overwhelming now; we'll cover the Control Center in more detail later.

Swipe Down from the Top Left Corner or the Middle of the Screen: This action opens the Notification Center, displaying your recent notifications and widgets. You'll get used to checking your notifications and managing them effectively as we progress.

The icons on your home screen serve as gateways to your apps. Tap an icon to open the corresponding app. You can organize these icons by pressing and holding on an app until they start to jiggle, then dragging them to your desired location. To create folders, drag one app icon over another. This can help keep your home screen tidy and make it easier to find your favorite apps.

Customizing your home screen is simple and can make your iPhone more user-friendly. To change your wallpaper, go to Settings, then Wallpaper, and choose from Apple's images or your photos. You can set different wallpapers for your home screen and lock screen, adding a personal touch to your device.

In addition to app icons, you can add widgets to your home screen. Widgets offer quick insights from your favorite apps without requiring you to open them. To add a widget, press and hold on an empty space on the home screen until the apps start to jiggle, then tap the plus sign in the upper left corner. Browse the available widgets, select one, and place it on your home screen. You can adjust its size and position to fit your layout. We will explore widgets in more detail later, ensuring you understand how to use them effectively.

The App Library, located to the right of your last home screen page, organizes all your apps into categories automatically. This feature helps you find apps quickly without cluttering your main home screen pages. Swipe left until you reach the App Library and tap on any app to open it, or use the search bar at the top for quick access. Don't worry if this seems complex now; we'll break it down step by step later in the book.

Understanding the icons and symbols on your iPhone is essential for efficient use. The status bar at the top shows essential information such as the time, battery level, Wi-Fi signal, and cellular signal strength. Icons like the airplane mode symbol, Bluetooth, and Do Not Disturb indicate the status of these features. Familiarizing yourself with these icons will help you quickly assess your iPhone's status at a glance.

By mastering these basic navigation and customization techniques, you'll be well on your way to making the most of your iPhone. Remember, each step you take will bring you closer to mastering this powerful tool. With a personalized and well-organized interface, accessing your favorite apps and features will become second nature, enhancing your overall user experience. And rest assured, this guide will provide detailed explanations and tips in every chapter to help you navigate and enjoy your new device confidently.

Essential Settings

Getting your iPhone set up with the right settings is crucial for a smooth and enjoyable experience. These initial steps will ensure your device is configured to meet your needs and preferences. We'll cover connecting to Wi-Fi, adjusting volume and brightness, and setting up your Apple ID, providing a foundation for using your iPhone effectively.

First, let's connect your iPhone to a Wi-Fi network. This step is important as it allows your iPhone to access the internet, download updates, and stay connected. To connect to Wi-Fi, go to **Settings > Wi-Fi**, and you'll see a list of available networks. Find your home Wi-Fi network in the list and tap on it. You'll be prompted to enter the password. If you don't know your Wi-Fi password, it's usually found on your router or provided by your internet service provider. Enter the password and tap **Join**. Once connected, a checkmark will appear next to your network name, indicating a successful connection.

Next, let's adjust the volume and brightness to suit your preferences. You can control the volume using the physical buttons on the left side of your iPhone. The top button raises the volume, while the bottom button lowers it. For more detailed volume settings, go to **Settings > Sounds & Haptics**. Here, you can adjust the ringer and alert volumes, choose vibration patterns, and even customize sounds for different alerts.

Adjusting the screen brightness can make your iPhone easier to see in different lighting conditions. To adjust the brightness, swipe down from the top right corner of the screen to open the Control Center. You'll see a brightness slider; move it up to increase brightness and down to decrease it. For more precise control, go to **Settings > Display & Brightness**. Here, you can also enable True Tone, which automatically adjusts the display based on the ambient lighting, and Night Shift, which reduces blue light exposure in the evening to help you sleep better.

Setting up your Apple ID is another essential step. Your Apple ID allows you to access Apple services like the App Store, iCloud, iMessage, and FaceTime. If you don't yet have an Apple ID, you can create one when setting up your device. Go to **Settings > Sign in to your iPhone** at the top. Follow the prompts to create a new Apple ID or sign in with your existing one. You'll need an email address and a password. Once your Apple ID is set up, make sure to enable iCloud to back up your data. This ensures that your photos, contacts, and other essential information are safely stored in the cloud and can be easily restored if needed.

These foundational settings are just the beginning. As you continue to use your iPhone, you'll discover many more features and settings that can enhance your experience!

Chapter 2

Basic Phone Functions

Making and Receiving Calls

To make a call, start by opening the Phone app, represented by a green icon with a white telephone receiver. Once in the app, you'll see several tabs at the bottom: **Favorites**, **Recents**, **Contacts**, **Keypad**, and **Voicemail**. To dial a number manually, tap on the **Keypad** tab. Use the on-screen numbers to enter the phone number you wish to call, then tap the green phone button to initiate the call.

If the person you want to call is already saved in your contacts, you can access them quickly. Tap the **Contacts** tab to view your list of saved contacts. Scroll through the list or use the search bar at the top to find the person you want to call. Once you find the contact, tap their name, then tap the phone icon next to their number to start the call.

When someone calls you, you will see their name or number displayed on the screen, along with options to **Accept** or **Decline** the call. To answer, simply tap the green **Accept** button. If you cannot take the call, tap the red **Decline** button to send the call to voicemail. Alternatively, you can press the side button on your iPhone to silence the ringing without declining the call, giving you a moment to decide whether to answer.

During a call, you have several options to manage the conversation. You can use the speakerphone by tapping the **Speaker** button or mute your microphone by tapping the **Mute** button. If you need to access other features or apps while on a call, you can swipe up from the bottom to return to the home screen. The call will continue, and you can return to the call screen by tapping the green bar at the top of the screen.

Voicemail is a handy feature for receiving messages when you're unable to answer a call. To set up your voicemail, open the Phone app and tap the **Voicemail** tab. Follow the prompts to create a voicemail password and record a greeting. Once set up, you can listen to your voicemails by tapping on the **Voicemail** tab and selecting the message you want to hear. Tap the play button to listen, and you can also delete or save messages as needed.

Your iPhone 15 also offers additional call features that can enhance your calling experience. For example, you can add a second call to create a conference call by tapping **Add Call** during an active call. This allows you to speak with multiple people simultaneously. You can also use the **Call Waiting** feature, which notifies you of an incoming call while you're already on another call. You'll have the option to hold the current call and answer the new one, ensuring you never miss important conversations.

Sending and Receiving Texts

Staying connected through text messaging is simple and efficient. The Messages app, represented by a green icon with a white speech bubble, allows you to send and receive text messages, photos, videos, and more.

To send a text message, open the **Messages** app and tap the compose button (a square with a pencil) in the top right corner. This will open a new message window. In the "To:" field, start typing the name or phone number of the person you want to message. If they are in your contacts, their name will appear as you type. Tap on the name to select the recipient. Next, tap on the text field at the bottom of the screen to start typing your message. Once you've composed your message, tap the blue arrow button to send it.

When someone sends you a text, you'll receive a notification on your iPhone. Swipe down from the top of the screen to view the notification and tap on it to open the message. Alternatively, open the **Messages** app to see a list of your conversations. Tap on a conversation to read and respond to messages.

Adding fun elements to your messages, like emojis and voice messages, is easy. To add an emoji, tap the smiley face icon on the keyboard while typing a message. This will open the emoji keyboard, where you can select from a variety of emojis to include in your message. To send a voice message, press and hold the microphone icon next to the text field, speak your message, and then let go of the icon to send it. These features can make your conversations more lively and personal.

Group messaging is another excellent feature of the Messages app. To start a group message, follow the same steps for composing a new message, but add multiple recipients in the "To:" field. This allows you to communicate with several people at once, making it easy to plan events or stay in touch with family and friends.

If you want to customize your messaging experience, the Messages app offers several settings. Go to **Settings > Messages** to explore options like enabling iMessage, turning on read receipts, and adjusting notification settings. iMessage allows you to send messages over Wi-Fi or cellular data to other Apple devices, often resulting in faster delivery and additional features like sending photos and videos.

With these tools and tips, sending and receiving texts on your iPhone will become a seamless part of your daily routine. Whether you're sharing a quick update, sending a photo, or planning an outing with friends, the Messages app provides a reliable and enjoyable way to stay in touch.

Managing Contacts

Efficiently managing your contacts ensures that you can easily stay connected with the important people in your life. The Contacts app, represented by a gray icon with an outline of a person, is your gateway to organizing and accessing contact information.

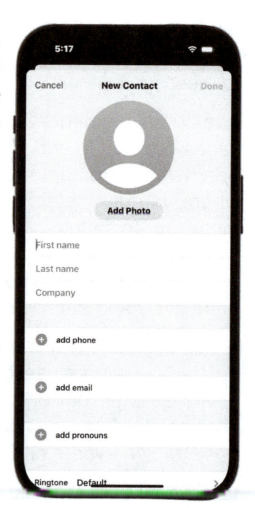

To add a new contact, open the **Contacts** app and tap the **+** button in the top right corner. This will bring up a form where you can enter the contact's details, such as their name, phone number, email address, and more. Once you've filled in the necessary information, tap **Done** to save the contact. Now, this person's details will be easily accessible whenever you need them.

Updating existing contacts is just as easy. Open the **Contacts** app and find the contact you wish to edit by scrolling through the list or using the search bar at the top. Tap on the contact's name to open their details, then tap **Edit** in the top right corner. Make the desired changes, such as updating a phone number or adding a new email address, and then tap **Done** to save the changes.

To delete a contact, open the **Contacts** app, find and tap on the contact you wish to remove, and then tap **Edit**. Scroll to the bottom of the contact's details and tap **Delete Contact**. Confirm your decision by tapping **Delete Contact** again. This will delete the contact from your list permanently.

Organizing your contacts can make it easier to find and connect with people quickly. You can create groups to categorize your contacts, such as family, friends, or work colleagues. To create a group, you'll need to use the **iCloud website** on a computer. Go to iCloud.com, sign in with your Apple ID, and select **Contacts**. Click on the **+** button at the bottom left and choose **New Group**. Name the group and then drag and drop contacts into it. These groups will sync to your iPhone, allowing you to quickly access specific sets of contacts.

The **Favorites** feature in the Phone app offers another way to quickly reach your most important contacts. To add someone to your Favorites, open the **Phone** app, go to the **Favorites** tab, and tap **+** in the top left corner. Select the contact you want to add and choose the type of communication (call, message, FaceTime) you prefer. This person will now appear in your Favorites list for easy access.

Chapter 3
Staying Connected

Using Email

Setting up and using email on your iPhone enabling you to stay in touch and manage your communications efficiently. The Mail app, represented by a blue icon with a white envelope, allows you to send, receive, and organize your emails with ease.

To set up your email account, go to **Settings > Mail > Accounts > Add Account**. Here, you will see a list of popular email providers such as iCloud, Google, Yahoo, and others. Tap on your email provider and follow the on-screen instructions to enter your email address and password. If your provider is not listed, select **Other** and manually enter your account details. Once your account is set up, your emails will start syncing to the Mail app.

To send an email, open the **Mail** app, and tap the compose button (a square with a pencil) in the bottom right corner. This will open a new email window. In the "To:" field, type the recipient's email address. If the person is in your contacts, their email address will appear as you type. Next, add a subject in the "Subject" field and then compose your message in the body section. When you're ready to send, tap the blue arrow button in the top right corner.

Receiving and reading emails is just as easy. When you receive a new email, you'll get a notification on your iPhone. Open the **Mail** app to see a list of your inbox messages. Tap on an email to open and read it. If you need to reply, tap the reply arrow at the bottom of the screen, compose your response, and tap the blue arrow button to send it.

Organizing your inbox helps keep your emails manageable. The Mail app offers several tools to help with this. To move an email to a different folder, swipe left on the email in your inbox and tap **Move**. Select the destination folder from the list. To delete an email, swipe left and tap **Delete**. You can also flag important emails by swiping right and tapping **Flag**. This helps you easily find and prioritize critical messages.

To manage multiple email, use the Mail app. You can add several accounts and view all your emails in one unified inbox, or switch between accounts by tapping on **Mailboxes** in the top left corner and selecting the desired account.

Customizing your email settings can enhance your experience. Go to **Settings > Mail** to adjust diverse options, such as setting up a signature, enabling notifications, and managing your accounts. For instance, you can create a custom signature that will automatically appear at the end of every email you send, adding a distinctive touch to your messages.

Browsing the Internet

Browsing the internet on iPhone is a straightforward and enjoyable experience with the Safari browser, represented by a blue compass icon. Whether you want to read the news, find a recipe, or explore new hobbies, Safari provides a fast, secure, and user-friendly way to explore the web. Getting started with Safari is easy, and with a few simple steps, you'll be navigating the internet like a pro. With the following tips and tools, browsing the internet on your iPhone 15 is a seamless experience. Whether you're searching for information, reading articles, or exploring new websites, Safari offers a robust and user-friendly platform to meet all your browsing needs.

To start browsing, open the **Safari** app. You'll see the address bar at the top of the screen where you can enter a web address (URL) or type keywords to search for information. For example, to visit a specific website, type the URL (e.g., www.example.com) and tap **Go**. To perform a search, type your keywords (e.g., "best gardening tips") and tap **Go** to see the search results.

To navigate through web pages, scroll up and down by swiping your finger on the screen. To go back to a previous page, tap the **Back** arrow in the bottom left corner. To go forward again, tap the **Forward** arrow next to it. If you want to refresh the page to see the latest content, tap the circular arrow icon in the address bar.

Using tabs in Safari allows you to keep multiple web pages open at the same time. To open a new tab, tap the **Tabs** button (two overlapping squares) in the bottom right corner, then tap the **+** button. This will open a new tab where you can enter a URL or search. To switch between tabs, tap the **Tabs** button again and select the tab you want to view. To close a tab, tap the **Tabs** button, then tap the **X** on the tab you want to close.

Bookmarking your favorite websites makes it easy to return to them later. To bookmark a page, tap the **Share** button (a square with an arrow pointing up) at the bottom of the screen, then tap **Add Bookmark**. You can choose to save the bookmark in your favorites or create a new folder to organize your bookmarks. To access your bookmarks, tap the **Bookmarks** button (an open book icon) at the bottom of the screen.

Reading content is made easier with Safari's Reader mode. When you open an article, you might see a **Reader** button in the address bar. Tap it to enter Reader mode, which strips away ads and oth-er distractions, leaving you with a clean, easy-to-read page. You can adjust the font size and background color in Reader mode to make read-ing more comfortable.

Privacy and security are important while browsing the internet. Safari offers features to protect your per-sonal information. For instance, you can enable Private Browsing to pre-vent Safari from saving your brows-ing history. To activate it, tap the **Tabs** button, then tap **Private** in the lower left corner, and tap **+** to open a new private tab. Additionally, Sa-fari's Intelligent Tracking Prevention helps block trackers from following you across websites, enhancing your privacy.

If you want to customize your brows-ing experience, go to **Settings >**

Safari. Here, you can adjust options such as search engine preferences, autofill settings, and privacy features. For example, you can choose your preferred search engine, enable or disable pop-up blockers, and manage your passwords for quick logins.

Video Calling with FaceTime

FaceTime is an effective way to maintain connections with loved ones through video calls. The app, represented by a green icon with a white video camera, allows you to make high-quality video and audio calls to anyone with an Apple device. Whether you're catching up with family, holding a virtual meeting, or sharing a special moment, FaceTime makes it easy to stay in touch.

To make a FaceTime call, start by opening the **FaceTime** app. Once the app is open, tap the **+** button in the top right corner. This will open a new call window where you can enter the name, email address, or phone number of the person you want to call. If the person is in your contacts, their name will appear as you type. Select the contact and then tap **Video** to start a video call or **Audio** to make an audio-only call.

When someone calls you on FaceTime, you will see an incoming call screen with the options to **Accept** or **Decline** the call. Tap the green Accept button to answer the call or tap the red Decline button to reject the call. If you're already on a FaceTime call and receive another call, you can choose to hold the current call and answer the new one, like managing regular phone calls.

During a FaceTime call, you have several features to enhance your experience. You can switch between the front and rear cameras by tapping the camera flip icon. This is useful if you want to show something around you to the person you're calling. You can also mute your microphone by tapping the **Mute** button, which allows you to listen without being heard. To end the call, tap the red **End** button.

Group FaceTime calls allow you to chat with multiple people simultaneously. To start a group FaceTime call, open the **FaceTime** app and tap the **+** button. Enter the names, email addresses, or phone numbers of the people you want to include in the call. Once you've added everyone, tap **Video** to start the group call. During a group FaceTime call, the active speaker's tile will enlarge automatically, making it easier to follow the conversation.

FaceTime also offers features like **Effects** and **Filters** to make your calls more fun and interactive. During a call, tap the star icon to access various effects, such as Animoji, Memoji, and different filters. These can add a playful element to your calls, making them more enjoyable, especially when talking with grandchildren or friends.

Chapter 4

Photos and Memories

Taking Photos

Capturing special moments has never been easier or more enjoyable than with the iPhone 15's advanced camera. As someone who cherishes family gatherings, scenic walks, and special events, having a reliable and powerful camera at your fingertips can make all the difference. The camera is designed to be user-friendly, allowing you to take stunning photos with just a few taps. Whether you're documenting precious moments with your grandchildren, capturing the beauty of your garden, or exploring new hobbies like photography, the iPhone is equipped to meet your needs. Let's explore how you can maximize the benefits of this fantastic feature.

To open the camera, simply tap the **Camera** app icon on your home screen. When the app opens, you'll see the viewfinder displaying what your camera sees. At the bottom of the screen, you'll find different modes such as **Photo**, **Portrait**, **Video**, and more. To take a standard photo, ensure you're in **Photo** mode by swiping left or right until it is highlighted.

Position your iPhone to frame your shot. You can tap on the screen to focus on a specific area, which will adjust the exposure and focus automatically. For more control, you can adjust the exposure manually by sliding your finger up or down on the screen after focusing. Once you're ready to take the photo, tap the white circle button at the bottom of the screen.

For portraits, use Portrait mode. This setting creates a professional depth effect by blurring the background while keeping the subject sharply focused. Position your subject within the frame and follow any on-screen instructions for optimal distance. When everything looks good, tap the shutter button to take the portrait photo.

Using the **Live Photos** feature can add a dynamic element to your pictures. Live Photos captures a few seconds of motion and sound around the moment you press the shutter button. To enable Live Photos, tap the circle icon with a dotted outline at the top of the screen until it turns yellow. Now, when you take a photo, it will include a short video clip that you can view by pressing and holding the photo in your gallery.

If you want to capture a wider scene, switch to **Panorama** mode by swiping through the camera modes. In **Panorama** mode, tap the shutter button and slowly move your iPhone horizontally. An arrow on the screen will guide you to keep the iPhone level as you move. Once you reach the end of your desired shot, tap the shutter button again to finish.

The iPhone 15 also offers various filters and editing tools to enhance your photos. After taking a photo, open the **Photos** app and select the image you want to edit. Tap **Edit** in the top right corner to access the editing tools. Here, you can adjust brightness, contrast, and color, or apply filters to change the look of your photo. Once you're satisfied with the edits, tap **Done** to save the changes.

For those interested in macro photography, the iPhone 15's advanced camera system allows you to capture intricate details up close. To take a macro photo, move your iPhone close to your subject. The camera will automatically switch to macro mode, adjusting the focus to capture the fine details.

Viewing and Managing Photos

Once you've taken your beautiful photos with the iPhone 15, it's time to view and manage them. The Photos app, represented by a colorful flower icon, is your hub for all your pictures and videos. It offers a range of features to help you organize, edit, and share your memories.

To view your photos, open the **Photos** app. The main screen, called the **Library**, displays all your photos and videos organized by date. You can scroll through your collection to revisit moments captured over time. If you're looking for a specific photo, use the search bar at the top to type keywords, dates, or locations to find exactly what you need.

Organizing your photos into albums makes it easier to find and enjoy them later. To create a new album, go to **Albums** at the bottom of the screen and tap the **+** button in the top left corner. Select **New Album**, give it a name, and then add the photos you want to include. You can always add more photos to the album later by tapping **Add Photos** within the album.

Editing your photos is straightforward with the powerful tools available in the Photos app. Select a photo you want to edit, then tap **Edit** in the top right corner. Here, you can adjust brightness, contrast, and color, apply filters, crop the image, and more. Use the adjustment sliders to fine-tune your photo to your liking. Once you're satisfied with the edits, tap **Done** to save your changes.

Creating memories with the **Memories** feature is a wonderful way to relive special occasions. Memories automatically curates photos and videos into short movies based on events, dates, or locations. To view a memory, go to the **For You** tab at the bottom of the screen and select one of the memory collections. You can customize these memories by changing the music, title, and length, making them perfect for sharing with family and friends.

To share your photos, tap on a photo or video you want to share, then tap the **Share** button (a square with an arrow pointing up). You can choose to send your photos via Messages, Mail, or social media apps like Facebook and Instagram. You can also create shared albums to collaborate with others. To create a shared album, go to **Albums**, tap the **+** button, select **New Shared Album**, and invite people to join. This way, everyone can contribute their photos and videos to the shared collection.

Backing Up Your Photos

Ensuring your photos are safely backed up is crucial for preserving your precious memories. With the iPhone 15, using iCloud to back up your photos is a simple and effective way to keep them secure. This process helps protect your pictures from being lost due to device damage or loss and ensures they are accessible from any Apple device.

To start backing up your photos with iCloud, go to **Settings > [your name] > iCloud > Photos** and turn on **iCloud Photos**. Enabling this feature will automatically upload and store your entire photo library in iCloud. Your photos and videos will sync across all your Apple devices, allowing you to access them anytime, anywhere. This means that any photo you take with your iPhone will be available on your iPad, Mac, or other devices linked to your Apple ID.

Managing your iCloud storage is crucial to make sure you have enough space for all your photos. iCloud offers 5GB of free storage, but you may need more if you have a large photo library. To check your current storage usage, go to **Settings > [your name] > iCloud > Manage Storage**. Here, you can see how much storage you have left and upgrade to a larger plan if needed. Apple offers various plans to suit different needs, and upgrading can provide ample space to store all your memories.

In addition to iCloud, there are other ways to back up your photos. One method is to use your computer. Connect your iPhone to your computer using a USB cable and open the **Photos** app on your Mac or **File Explorer** on your Windows PC. Import your photos to your computer, creating a secondary backup that can be especially useful if you prefer to have a local copy of your files.

Another backup option is using third-party cloud storage services like Google Photos, Dropbox, or OneDrive. These services offer additional storage options and can be used alongside iCloud. To use these services, download the respective app from the App Store, sign in or create an account, and follow the instructions to upload your photos. These platforms often provide features such as automatic backups and easy sharing options, adding another layer of security for your photos.

Regularly backing up your photos is important for keeping your memories safe. Set reminders to check your backups periodically and ensure everything is up to date. This habit will help you avoid the stress of losing irreplaceable photos and keep your digital memories well-organized and secure.

Chapter 5

Keeping Track of Time and Tasks

Using the Clock App

The Clock app on your new iPhone is a versatile tool that helps you manage time efficiently. Whether you need to set alarms, use the timer, or track different time zones, the Clock app has you covered. Represented by a black icon with a white clock face, this app is designed to make your daily schedule more manageable.

To get started, open the **Clock** app from your home screen. The app has several functions: **World Clock**, **Alarm**, **Bedtime**, **Stopwatch**, and **Timer**, each accessible through the tabs at the bottom of the screen.

Setting an alarm is straightforward. Tap the **Alarm** tab, then tap the **+** button in the top right corner. Use the scroll wheels to set the desired time for your alarm, then tap **Save**. You can customize the alarm by setting a label, choosing a sound, and enabling the snooze option. Labels can be helpful reminders of why you set the alarm, such as "Take medication" or "Pick up grandchildren."

The **World Clock** feature allows you to keep track of time in different parts of the world. This is particularly useful if you have family or friends in different time zones. To add a new city, tap the **World Clock** tab, then tap the **+** button in the top right corner. Type the name of the city you want to add and select it from the list. The app will display the current time for that location, making it easy to coordinate calls or meetings across time zones.

Using the **Timer** is helpful for various tasks, such as cooking or exercising. To set a timer, tap the **Timer** tab, use the scroll wheels to set the desired duration, and tap **Start**. The timer will count down and alert you when the time is up. You can customize the timer sound by tapping **When Timer Ends** and selecting a different alert tone.

The Stopwatch feature is ideal for timing activities or events. To use the stopwatch, tap the **Stopwatch** tab, then tap **Start** to begin timing. Tap **Lap** to record lap times without stopping the overall timer. When you're done, tap **Stop** and then **Reset** to clear the stopwatch.

For a good night's sleep, use the **Sleep** feature in the **Health** app to establish a regular sleep schedule. To set it up, open the **Health** app, tap **Browse**, then tap **Sleep**. Follow the on-screen instructions to choose your desired wake-up time and how many hours of sleep you need. The app will remind you when it's time to go to bed and wake you up gently in the morning. You can track your sleep patterns and adjust your schedule as needed to improve your sleep habits.

Staying Organized with the Calendar

Keeping track of important dates and events is a breeze with the Calendar app. The app, represented by a white icon with a red header and the current date, helps you manage your schedule efficiently. Whether you're planning family gatherings, medical appointments, or social activities, the Calendar app ensures you never miss an important event.

To get started, open the **Calendar** app from your home screen. The app displays your calendar in different views, including **Day**, **Week**, **Month**, and **Year**. You can switch between these views by tapping the corresponding tab at the bottom of the screen. The **Month** view is particularly useful for getting an overview of your upcoming events.

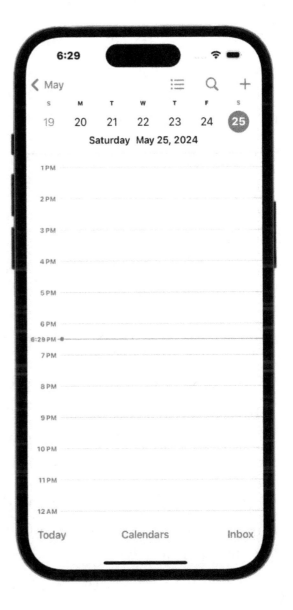

To add a new event, tap the **+** button in the top right corner of the screen. Enter the event title, location, and start and end times. If it's an all-day event, toggle the **All-day** switch. You can also set a repeat schedule for recurring events, such as weekly meetings or monthly appointments. To add a reminder, tap **Alert** and choose when you'd like to be notified before the event. Once you've entered all the details, tap **Add** to save the event to your calendar.

Editing or deleting events is simple. Tap on the event in your calendar to open its details, then tap **Edit** in the top right corner. Make the necessary changes and tap **Done** to save the updates. To delete the event, scroll to the bottom of the screen and tap **Delete Event**.

The Calendar app also allows you to create multiple calendars to organize your events by category. For example, you might have separate calendars for family activities, work, and personal appointments. To create a new calendar, open the Calendar app, tap **Calendars** at the bottom, then tap **Add Calendar**. Once created, you can assign events to specific calendars by selecting the calendar during event creation.

Sharing your calendar with others is a fantastic way to coordinate schedules. To share a calendar, open the **Calendar** app, tap **Calendars** at the bottom, then tap the **i** icon next to the calendar you want to share. Tap **Add Person** and enter the email address of the person you want to share with. They will receive an invitation to view and edit your calendar, making it easier to stay in sync with family and friends.

The **Calendar** app integrates seamlessly with other apps on your iPhone, such as **Mail** and **Contacts**. If you receive an event invitation via email, you can easily add it to your calendar with a single tap. Additionally, events can be linked to contacts, allowing you to see who's attending and contact them directly from the event details.

Customizing your calendar settings helps you tailor the app to your needs. Go to **Settings > Calendar** to adjust diverse options, such as default alert times, time zone support, and calendar colors. These settings ensure your calendar is personalized and easy to navigate.

Using Notes and Reminders

The Notes and Reminders apps on your iPhone 15 are indispensable tools for organizing your daily life, capturing ideas, and managing tasks. For someone who enjoys a busy and fulfilling life, these apps can help keep track of everything from shopping lists to important appointments. Imagine planning a family gathering, keeping track of medical appointments, or simply jotting down a brilliant idea that comes to you during a walk in the garden. The Notes and Reminders apps are designed to fit seamlessly into your lifestyle, ensuring that you never miss a beat.

To begin with the **Notes** app, represented by a yellow and white icon, open it from your home screen. Creating a new note is easy—tap the **New Note** button, which looks like a square with a pencil, in the bottom right corner. Start typing your thoughts, ideas, or lists. For instance, you might use Notes to jot down a recipe you plan to try, make a list of books you want  to read, or keep a record of your gardening tips. You can also add photos, sketches, and even scanned documents to your notes by tapping the **Camera** icon above the keyboard. This flexibility makes Notes a versatile tool for capturing information in various formats, whether you're documenting your volunteer activities or creating a to-do list for your part-time job.

You can organize related notes by creating folders. To create a folder, go to the **Notes** main screen, tap the **<** button in the top left corner, then tap **New Folder** at the bottom. Name the folder and tap **Save**. You might create separate folders for various aspects of your life, such as "Family," "Health," "Hobbies," and "Travel." You can move existing notes into folders by swiping left on the note, tapping **Move**, and selecting the desired folder.

To share notes, open the note you want to share, tap the **Share** button (a square with an arrow pointing up), and choose how you'd like to share it. You can send notes via Messages, Mail, or other apps installed on your iPhone. This feature is especially useful for collaborating on lists or sharing important information with family members. For example, you can share a shopping list with your spouse or send a travel itinerary to your children.

The **Reminders** app, represented by a white icon with colored dots, helps you manage tasks and to-do lists effectively. To create a new reminder, open the app and tap **New Reminder** in the lower left corner. Enter the task description and set a due date and time by tapping the **i** button next to the reminder. You can also add notes and priority levels to your reminders, making it easy to manage and prioritize your tasks. For example, you can set a reminder to take your medication at a specific time each day or create a list of tasks to complete for an upcoming community event you're organizing.

Organizing reminders into lists helps keep your tasks structured. To create a new list, tap **Add List** at the bottom of the main screen, choose a color and icon, and name your list. You can add reminders to specific lists by selecting the list and tapping **New Reminder**. This way, you can have separate lists for groceries, work tasks, and personal projects. Imagine having a "Gardening" list for all the tasks you want  to complete in your garden, a "Travel" list for packing items and itinerary details, and a "Volunteer" list for the activities you're involved in at your local community center.

Setting location-based reminders is another powerful feature. To do this, create a new reminder or edit an existing one, tap the **i** button, and enable **Remind me at a location**. Enter the address or choose from your saved locations. Your iPhone will alert you when you arrive or leave the specified location, ensuring you don't forget important tasks while you're out. For instance, you can set a reminder to pick up groceries when you arrive at the supermarket, or to call a friend when you leave a specific location.

Both apps offer integration with Siri for hands-free convenience. You can create notes and reminders using voice commands by saying, "Hey Siri, create a note" or "Hey Siri, remind me to..." followed by your task. This feature is particularly useful when your hands are full or you're on the go. Imagine you're cooking and need to add an item to your shopping list—just ask Siri, and it's done without missing a beat in your recipe.

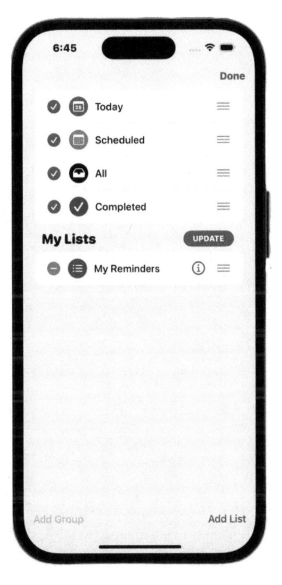

Chapter 6

Health and Wellness

Using the Health App

The Health app is a powerful tool designed to help you monitor and manage your wellness. For someone who values staying active and healthy, this app provides a comprehensive way to track various aspects of your health. Whether you're managing a health condition, staying fit, or simply want to keep a closer eye on your well-being, the Health app is tailored to support your needs.

Imagine you start your day with a morning walk. The Health app can track your steps, distance, and calories burned, giving you a clear picture of your daily activity. To get started, open the **Health** app, represented by a white icon with a red heart. When you open the app for the first time, you'll be prompted to set up your health profile. This involves entering basic information such as your age, weight, height, and other relevant details. This profile helps the app provide more accurate data and insights tailored to your needs.

The **Summary** tab is your main dashboard, where you can view a snapshot of your health data. Here, you can see your activity levels, heart rate, and other key metrics immediately. For example, if you enjoy gardening, you can track the amount of time you spend being active outside. Tap on any metric to view more detailed information and trends over time. This helps you understand your activity patterns and make adjustments if needed.

To track specific health metrics, you can add them to your favorites. Go to the **Browse** tab, where you'll find a list of health categories such as **Activity**, **Heart**, **Sleep**, and **Mindfulness**. Tap on a category to explore the available metrics, then tap the **Add to Favorites** button to include them in your Summary tab. This customization allows you to focus on the metrics that matter most to you. For instance, if you're monitoring your heart health, you can keep an eye on your resting heart rate and heart rate variability.

One of the standout features of the Health app is its ability to integrate with other health and fitness devices and apps. If you have an Apple Watch or other compatible devices, you can sync them with the Health app to get a more comprehensive view of your health. For example, your Apple Watch can track your workouts, measure your heart rate, and even monitor your sleep patterns. All this data is seamlessly integrated into the Health app, giving you a holistic view of your wellness.

The Health app also supports the integration of third-party apps. To connect these apps, go to **Settings > Health > Data Access & Devices**. Here, you can see a list of apps that are compatible with the Health app and choose which ones to sync. This feature is particularly useful if you use specific apps for tracking nutrition, meditation, or other health-related activities. For instance, a nutrition app can log your daily food intake and sync it with the Health app, helping you monitor your diet alongside your physical activity.

Setting up health notifications can help you stay on top of your wellness goals. To enable notifications, go to **Settings > Notifications > Health** and turn on the notifications you want to receive. These alerts can remind you to stand, move, breathe, or take medication, ensuring you stay engaged with your health throughout the day. Imagine getting a gentle reminder to take a short walk after sitting for a while or a prompt to practice mindfulness exercises in the afternoon.

The **Health Records** feature allows you to consolidate your medical information in one place. If your healthcare provider supports Health Records on iPhone, you can securely download your medical records, including lab results, immunizations, and medications, directly into the Health app. To set this up, go to the **Browse** tab, tap **Health Records**, and follow the prompts to connect with your healthcare provider. This feature provides easy access to your medical history, which can be invaluable during medical appointments or emergencies. For example, if you have a doctor's appointment, you can quickly pull up your latest lab results or a list of your medications.

For those focused on fitness, the Health app offers detailed workout tracking. Whether you're walking, swimming, or doing yoga, you can log your workouts and see detailed metrics on your performance. This helps you track your progress and stay motivated to reach your fitness goals. Imagine seeing a month's worth of yoga sessions and noticing your flexibility and endurance improve over time.

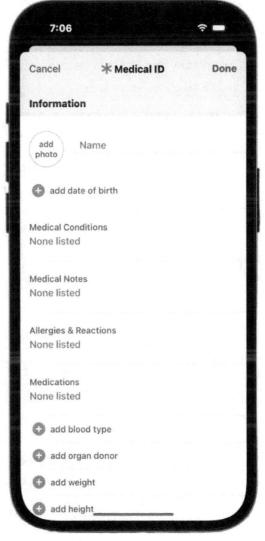

Fitness and Activity Tracking

Staying active is crucial for maintaining your health and well-being, and the iPhone 15, along with the Apple

Watch, offers a range of features to help you track your fitness and activities. Imagine beginning your day with a morning walk, then doing some gardening, and later playing with your grandchildren. These activities not only keep you physically fit but also bring joy and satisfaction to your daily routine. The Fitness app on your iPhone and the Apple Watch are designed to seamlessly integrate into your lifestyle, making it easier to monitor and encourage your physical activity.

The **Fitness** app on your iPhone, represented by a red icon with a white ring, is the central hub for all your activity data. To get started, open the **Fitness** app. Here, you'll see your Activity Rings: **Move**, **Exercise**, and **Stand**. These rings provide a visual representation of your daily activity goals and help you stay motivated to move more, exercise regularly, and avoid prolonged sitting.

The **Move** ring tracks your active calories burned throughout the day. This feature is particularly useful if you enjoy activities like gardening, walking, or playing with your grandchildren. For example, each time you take a walk around your neighborhood, engage in a gardening session, or play a game of tag with your grandkids, your Move ring will gradually close, giving you a sense of accomplishment.

The **Exercise** ring tracks your minutes of brisk activity. You can complete this ring by doing any form of exercise, whether it's a structured workout or simply a brisk walk. Imagine setting aside time each day for a yoga session or a vigorous walk in the park. The goal is to reach at least 30 minutes of exercise each day, and as you engage in these activities, you'll see the Exercise ring close, reflecting your efforts.

The **Stand** ring encourages you to stand up and move for at least one minute during 12 different hours of the day. This is especially important if you find yourself sitting for long periods, such as while reading or watching TV. Your iPhone or Apple Watch will send gentle reminders to stand and move, improving circulation and lowering the risks associated with sitting for long periods. Even a brief stroll around your living room can help close this ring.

For more detailed tracking, you can use the **Workout** app on the Apple Watch. This app offers various workout types, such as walking, running, cycling, swimming, and even yoga. To start a workout, open the **Workout** app on your watch, select the type of workout, and tap **Start**. The watch will track your duration, calories burned, heart rate, and other metrics relevant to the workout. For example, if you decide to go for a swim at the local pool, the Workout app will monitor your performance and sync this data with the **Fitness** app on your iPhone, providing a comprehensive view of your activity.

If you prefer tracking your workouts without an Apple Watch, you can still log activities manually. In the **Fitness** app on your iPhone, tap the **+** button in the upper right corner, select **Add Workout**, and enter the details of your activity. This allows you to keep track of exercises like stretching routines or home workouts that might not be automatically detected.

Activity challenges and competitions can also be a fun way to stay motivated. You can share your activity data with friends and family and participate in challenges to see who can close their rings first. To share your activity, open the **Fitness** app, tap the **Sharing** tab, and follow the prompts to add friends. Imagine setting up a friendly competition with your family members to see who can reach their activity goals each week. This social aspect can add extra motivation and make fitness more enjoyable.

The **Trends** feature in the **Fitness** app helps you understand your long-term activity patterns. By tracking your trends over time, you can see whether you're increasing your activity levels or if there are areas that need improvement. For example, you might notice that you've been consistently meeting your exercise goals but need to work on standing up more frequently throughout the day. This insight can help you set realistic goals and make informed decisions about your fitness routine.

Accessibility Features

The iPhone 15 is equipped with a wide range of accessibility features designed to make the device easier to use for everyone, including those with vision, hearing, motor, or cognitive impairments. These features ensure that you can customize your iPhone to suit your individual needs, making everyday tasks more manageable and enhancing your overall experience.

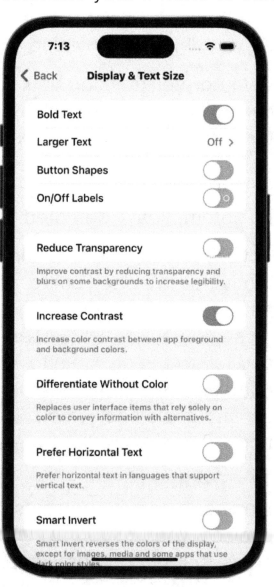

For users with vision impairments, the iPhone offers several helpful tools. The **VoiceOver** feature is a screen reader that provides spoken descriptions of what's on your screen. To enable VoiceOver, go to **Settings > Accessibility > Voice-Over** and toggle it on. With VoiceOver activated, you can use gestures to hear descriptions of what you touch on the screen, from icons to text, helping you navigate your iPhone with greater ease.

Zoom is another useful feature that magnifies the screen, making text and images larger and easier to see. To turn on Zoom, go to **Settings >**

Accessibility > Zoom and toggle it on. You can adjust the zoom level by double-tapping with three fingers and dragging up or down. This feature is particularly beneficial when reading small print or viewing detailed images.

For users who need larger text, the iPhone allows you to adjust the font size system wide. Go to **Settings > Accessibility > Display & Text Size > Larger Text** and use the slider to increase the text size. This adjustment applies to most apps and makes reading text messages, emails, and other content much more comfortable.

The **Magnifier** feature turns your iPhone into a digital magnifying glass, using the camera to help you see objects up close. To access the Magnifier, go to **Settings > Accessibility > Magnifier** and turn it on. Once enabled, you can triple-click the side button to open the Magnifier and use it to read fine print or view small objects in greater detail.

For users with hearing impairments, the iPhone offers several features to enhance audio accessibility. **Live Listen** uses your iPhone's microphone to amplify sound directly to your hearing aids or AirPods. To use Live Listen, go to **Settings > Accessibility > Hearing Devices** and connect your compatible hearing aids or AirPods. Then, open the **Control Center**, tap the hearing icon, and turn on Live Listen. This feature is useful in noisy environments or during conversations.

The **Sound Recognition** feature alerts you to specific sounds such as doorbells, alarms, and even a baby crying. To enable Sound Recognition, go to **Settings > Accessibility > Sound Recognition** and toggle it on. You can customize which sounds you want your iPhone to recognize, providing you with timely notifications when those sounds are detected.

For those with motor impairments, the iPhone includes features like **AssistiveTouch**, which allows you to perform actions that would typically require physical buttons. To enable AssistiveTouch, go to **Settings > Accessibility > Touch > AssistiveTouch** and toggle it on. This feature adds a floating menu on your screen with options like Home, Siri, Notifications, and more, making it easier to navigate your iPhone with minimal physical effort.

Voice Control lets you operate your iPhone using only your voice. To set up Voice Control, go to **Settings > Accessibility > Voice Control** and toggle it on. You can use voice commands to open apps, adjust settings, type text, and more. This feature is particularly helpful if you have difficulty using touch gestures or physical buttons.

The **Switch Control** feature allows you to control your iPhone using external switches or other adaptive devices. To set up Switch Control, go to **Settings > Accessibility > Switch Control** and follow the prompts to configure your switches. This feature is designed to provide greater independence for users with significant motor impairments.

Chapter 7

Exploring Apps and Games

Finding Apps in the App Store

The App Store is a treasure trove of applications that can enhance your daily life, from staying connected with loved ones to pursuing hobbies and managing tasks. Represented by a blue icon with a white "A," the App Store provides access to millions of apps designed to make your iPhone even more powerful and versatile.

To explore the App Store, tap the **App Store** icon on your home screen. Once inside, you'll find several tabs at the bottom: **Today**, **Games**, **Apps**, **Arcade**, and **Search**. Each tab offers a unique way to discover new and popular apps.

The **Today** tab features curated content, including app recommendations, developer stories, and tips on using various apps. This section is updated daily, providing fresh ideas and highlighting interesting apps you might not have discovered otherwise. For example, you might find an app that helps you learn a new language or one that offers guided meditation sessions to help you relax.

In the **Apps** tab, you'll find categories like Productivity, Health & Fitness, and Entertainment. Browsing these categories can help you find apps tailored to your interests and needs. If you enjoy cooking, you might explore the Food & Drink category for recipes and meal planning apps. If you're into reading, check out the Books category for eBook readers and audiobooks.

The **Search** tab allows you to find specific apps by typing keywords or the app's name into the search bar. This is particularly useful if you already know what you're looking for. For example, if you want an app to help you track your fitness goals, you can type "fitness tracker" to see a list of relevant apps. Tap on an app to view its details, including descriptions, screenshots, reviews, and ratings.

To download an app, tap the **Get** button next to the app's name. If the app has a price, the button will display the cost instead. You may need to enter your Apple ID password or use Face ID/Touch ID to confirm the download. After downloading, the app will appear on your home screen, ready for use.

The **Games** tab is dedicated to gaming apps, offering a wide range of games from puzzles to action-packed adventures. If you enjoy playing games in your leisure time, this tab is the perfect place to discover new titles and genres. You can find games that suit your interests, whether you prefer casual games to pass the time or more complex games that challenge your skills.

The **Arcade** tab provides access to Apple Arcade, a subscription service that offers unlimited access to a curated collection of premium games. These games are ad-free and do not require in-app purchases, providing a seamless gaming experience. To explore Apple Arcade, tap the **Arcade** tab and browse the available games. You can start a free trial to see if the service suits your gaming preferences.

Managing your downloaded apps is easy. To update your apps, go to the **Today** tab and tap your profile picture in the top right corner. Scroll down to see a list of apps with available updates and tap **Up-**

date All to keep your apps up to date. Regular updates ensure that your apps have the latest features and security improvements.

You can also organize your apps by creating folders on your home screen. To create a folder, press and hold an app icon until it starts to jiggle, then drag it over another app you want to include in the folder. Release the app, and a new folder will be created. You can rename the folder by tapping the name field. This is a great way to keep your home screen tidy and make it easier to find the apps you use most frequently.

Playing Games

Playing games can be a delightful way to pass the time, stay mentally sharp, and enjoy some fun. The App Store offers a vast selection of games across various genres, ensuring there's something for everyone, whether you prefer puzzle games, action-packed adventures, or relaxing casual games.

To start exploring games, open the **App Store** and tap on the **Games** tab at the bottom of the screen. Here, you'll find a curated collection of popular and trending games. You can browse through various categories like Adventure, Puzzle, Strategy, and more to find games that match your interests. For instance, if you enjoy solving puzzles, you might explore games like Sudoku, crosswords, or brain teasers that challenge your mind.

Once you find a game that piques your interest, tap on it to view more details. You'll see screenshots, descriptions, user reviews, and ratings that can help you decide if the game is right for you. To download the game, tap the **Get** button (or the price if it's a paid game) and confirm the download with your Apple ID password or Face ID/Touch ID. The game will appear on your home screen once the download is complete.

For those who enjoy a seamless gaming experience, consider exploring **Apple Arcade**. This subscription service offers unlimited access to a curated collection of premium games. The **Arcade** tab in the App Store lets you browse and discover new games without worrying about ads or in-app purchases. Games like "What the Golf?" or "Mini Motorways" offer unique and engaging experiences that can keep you entertained for hours.

To enhance your gaming experience, many games support **Game Center**, Apple's social gaming network. By signing into **Game Center**, you can track your high scores, compete on leaderboards, and earn achievements. To access Game Center, go to **Settings > Game Center** and sign in with your Apple ID. Once signed in, you can see your friends' activities and challenge them to beat your scores in your favorite games.

In addition to traditional games, your iPhone 15 supports **Augmented Reality (AR)** games, which blend digital content with the real world. AR games use your iPhone's camera and sensors to create immersive experiences. For example, games like "Pokémon GO" allow you to catch virtual creatures in your real-world environment, adding a layer of excitement to your daily walks.

If you prefer a more laid-back gaming experience, there are many casual games available. Games like "Candy Crush Saga" or "FarmVille 3" offer light-hearted fun that you can play at your own pace. These games often include social features, allowing you to connect with friends and family, share your progress, and help each other advance through the game.

Managing your games is easy. To keep them organized, you can create folders on your home screen. For example, you might create a folder named "Games" and place all your downloaded games inside. To create a folder, press and hold an app icon until it starts to jiggle, then drag it over another app you want to include in the folder. Release the app, and a new folder will be created. You can rename the folder by tapping the name field.

Updates for your games are important to ensure you have the latest features and bug fixes. To update your games, open the **App Store**, tap on your profile picture in the top right corner, and scroll down to see a list of apps with available updates. Tap **Update All** to download the latest versions.

Staying Informed with News Apps

The App Store offers a variety of news apps that cater to different interests, from general news to specialized topics like technology, sports, or finance. These apps ensure that you have access to the latest news at your fingertips, helping you stay updated and engaged with the world around you.

To find news apps, open the **App Store** and tap on the **Search** tab. Type in keywords like "news," "current events," or specific interests like "sports news" or "tech news." You will see a list of relevant apps that you can explore. Popular news apps include **Apple News**, **CNN**, **BBC News**, **The New York Times**, and **Reuters**.

Apple News is a built-in app that offers a comprehensive collection of news stories from various sources. To open Apple News, look for the app icon on your home screen, represented by a red "N" on a white background. Once inside, the **Today** tab shows a curated selection of top stories, trending topics, and personalized recommendations based on your interests. You can read full articles, watch news videos, and explore various categories such as politics, health, and entertainment.

To customize your news feed in Apple News, tap the **Following** tab at the bottom of the screen. Here, you can select the channels and topics you're interested in. Tap the **+** button next to a channel or topic to follow it. This ensures that your news feed is tailored to your preferences, making it easier to find stories that matter to you.

For those who prefer news from specific sources, downloading individual news apps can be beneficial. For instance, if you're a fan of sports, apps like **ESPN** or **Bleacher Report** provide in-depth coverage, live scores, and analysis. If you're interested in financial news, apps like **Bloomberg** or **CNBC** offer market updates, investment advice, and economic analysis.

Many news apps also offer features like notifications and breaking news alerts, ensuring you never miss important updates. To enable notifications, go to **Settings > Notifications**, select the news app, and turn on **Allow Notifications**. You can customize the notification settings to receive alerts for specific topics like politics, weather, or breaking news.

Reading the news on your iPhone is a convenient and flexible experience. You can adjust the text size in most news apps for better readability. In Apple News, go to **Settings > News** and use the slider to increase or decrease the font size. This makes reading articles more comfortable, especially for those who prefer larger text.

Sharing interesting news articles with friends and family is a breeze. In any news app, open the article you want to share, tap the **Share** button (a square with an arrow pointing up), and choose how you'd like to share it. You can send articles via Messages, Mail, or social media platforms, allowing you to discuss and share insights with others.

For those who enjoy in-depth analysis and long-form journalism, many news apps offer subscription services. Subscribing to services like **The New York Times** or **The Washington Post** provides access to premium content, including investigative reports, opinion pieces, and exclusive articles. Subscriptions often come with additional features like offline reading, ad-free browsing, and access to archives.

With the variety of news apps available, keeping up with global events has never been more convenient. Whether you prefer a broad overview of daily news or deep dives into specific topics, these apps provide the tools you need to stay up-to-date and engaged with the latest developments.

Chapter 8
Reading and Listening

Using the Books App

The Books app is a fantastic tool for those who love to read. Whether you prefer eBooks or audiobooks, this app offers a vast library of titles across all genres. It's perfect for enjoying your favorite stories, learning new things, or simply relaxing with a good book.

To get started, open the **Books** app, represented by an orange icon with a white book. Upon opening the app, you'll land on the **Reading Now** tab, which provides quick access to the books you are currently reading. This tab also offers recommendations based on your reading habits, making it easy to discover new books that match your interests.

To explore the vast selection of available books, tap on the **Book Store** tab at the bottom of the screen. Here, you can browse through various categories such as Bestsellers, New Releases, and Top Charts. If you have a specific book in mind, use the **Search** tab to find it quickly by typing the title, author, or a keyword.

When you find a book you want to buy, tap on its cover to view more details, including a summary, customer reviews, and a sample preview. If you decide to purchase the book, tap the price button and confirm the purchase with your Apple ID password or Face ID/ Touch ID. The book will then download to your library, ready for you to start reading.

If you enjoy listening to books, the Books app also features a wide range of audiobooks. Tap the **Audiobooks** tab to explore popular and recommended audiobooks. Just like with eBooks, you can purchase and download audiobooks to enjoy them on the go. Audiobooks are perfect for multitasking—whether you're driving, gardening, or simply relaxing at home.

To read a book, go to the **Library** tab, where you'll see all your purchased books and audiobooks. Tap on the cover of the book you want to read to open it. The reading interface is user-friendly, with options to adjust the font size and style, change the background color for better readability, and enable scrolling view if you prefer scrolling through the text instead of swiping pages.

The **Bookmark** feature allows you to save your place or mark important passages. To add a bookmark, tap the top-right corner of the page. You can access all your bookmarks later by tapping the **Bookmarks** icon in the top right corner of the screen. This is particularly useful if you want to return to specific parts of the book for reference or further reading.

The **Books** app also includes a **Note-taking** feature, which is handy for readers who like to jot down thoughts or highlight important sections. To highlight text, press and hold on a word, then drag to select the passage. Tap **Highlight** and choose a color. To add a note, select the text, tap **Note**, and type your thoughts. You can review all your highlights and notes by tapping the **Table of Contents** icon and selecting **Notes**.

For a hands-free reading experience, use the **Read Aloud** feature. With this option, your iPhone will read the text to you, which can be particularly helpful if you have difficulty reading small text or prefer to listen rather than read. To enable this feature, go to **Settings > Accessibility > Spoken Content** and turn on **Speak Screen**. Swipe down with two fingers from the top of the screen while in a book to activate the read-aloud function.

By utilizing the Books app, you can enjoy a rich reading experience, whether you're diving into the latest novel, exploring new genres, or listening to your favorite audiobooks. This app provides a convenient and enjoyable way to immerse yourself in literature wherever you are.

Listening to Music and Podcasts

Enjoying music and podcasts on your iPhone is a fantastic way to stay entertained, informed, and relaxed. With apps like Apple Music and Apple Podcasts, you have access to a vast library of songs and episodes that cater to every taste and interest.

To get started with **Apple Music**, open the **Music** app, represented by a white icon with a pink musical note. If you're new to Apple Music, you may need to sign up for a subscription, which gives you access to millions of songs, curated playlists, and radio stations. Once subscribed, you can explore the **Listen Now** tab, which provides personalized recommendations based on your listening habits. You'll find playlists, albums, and new releases tailored to your preferences.

To search for specific songs, artists, or albums, tap the **Search** tab at the bottom of the screen. Type in your query, and Apple Music will display relevant results. Tap on a song or album to start listening. If you find something you love, you can add it to your **Library** by tapping the **+ Add** button. This allows you to access your favorite music anytime easily.

Creating playlists is an excellent way to organize your music. To create a playlist, go to the **Library** tab, tap **Playlists**, and then **New Playlist**. Give your playlist a name and description, then tap **Add Music** to start adding songs. You can create playlists for different moods, activities, or occasions, such as "Relaxing Evenings," "Workout Tunes," or "Family Gatherings."

For those who enjoy discovering new music, the **Browse** tab is the place to go. Here, you'll find new releases, top charts, and curated playlists from Apple Music editors. The **Radio** tab lets you listen to live radio stations, including Apple Music 1, which features exclusive shows and interviews with artists.

Listening to podcasts is just as effortless with the Apple Podcasts app, represented by a purple icon with a white microphone. Open the app to explore a vast collection of podcasts on several topics, from news and true crime to comedy and education. The **Listen Now** tab provides personalized recommendations and highlights popular shows.

To find specific podcasts, use the **Search** tab and type in keywords or the name of the podcast. Tap on a show to view its episodes, read descriptions, and see reviews. To subscribe to a podcast, tap the **+ Subscribe** button, and new episodes will automatically download to your **Library**.

Managing your podcast episodes is simple. In the **Library** tab, you'll see all your subscribed shows and downloaded episodes. Tap on a show to view its episodes and select one to start listening. You can also create custom playlists of your favorite episodes by tapping **New Playlist** and adding episodes from different shows.

Both music and podcasts can be played through your iPhone's built-in speakers, connected headphones, or Bluetooth speakers. To adjust playback settings, such as volume and playback speed for podcasts, use the controls on the playback screen. For podcasts, you can also skip forward or backward by 15 seconds using the skip buttons.

Sharing your favorite songs and podcast episodes with friends and family is easy. In either the Music or Podcasts app, tap the **Share** button (a square with an arrow pointing up) and choose how you want to share the content. You can send it via Messages, Mail, or social media platforms.

Watching Videos

Watching videos on iPhone is a fantastic way to enjoy movies, TV shows, and other video content wherever you are. With the Apple TV app and other video streaming services, you have access to a vast library of entertainment options.

To start, open the **Apple TV** app, represented by a black icon with a white "TV" on it. The **Watch Now** tab offers a personalized selection of movies and TV shows based on your viewing habits. You can continue watching shows you've already started or find new recommendations tailored to your tastes.

If you're looking for something specific, use the **Search** tab at the bottom of the screen. Type in the name of a movie, TV show, or actor to find relevant content. When you find something you want to watch, tap on it to see more details, such as a summary, cast information, and trailers. To start watching, tap the **Play** button. If the content is not available for free, you can rent or purchase it by tapping the **Rent** or **Buy** button.

The **Library** tab in the Apple TV app contains all the movies and TV shows you've purchased or rented. You can also access your subscriptions to streaming services like Apple TV+, HBO Max, and Disney+ from here. To add a new subscription service, go to the **Watch Now** tab, scroll down to the **Channels** section, and tap on the service you want to subscribe to. Follow the prompts to sign up and start watching.

For those who enjoy live TV and sports, the **Apple TV** app also provides access to live broadcasts. Tap the **Sports** tab to see a list of live games and upcoming events. You can customize your sports preferences by selecting your favorite teams and leagues, ensuring you never miss a game.

Streaming services like **Netflix**, **Amazon Prime Video**, and **You-Tube** offer additional video content. Download these apps from the **App Store** and sign in with your account credentials to start watching. Each app has its own library of movies, TV shows, and original content. For example, Netflix offers a wide range of genres, from drama and comedy to documentaries and animated series.

To make your viewing experience more enjoyable, the iPhone 15 supports **HDR (High Dynamic Range)** video, which provides enhanced contrast and color. Many streaming services offer HDR content, which will automatically play in HDR if your iPhone supports it.

You can also download videos for offline viewing. In the **Apple TV** app, find the movie or TV show you want to download, then tap the **Download** button. This feature proves especially handy when you're traveling or in places with limited internet access. To access your downloaded content, go to the **Library** tab and select **Downloaded**.

If you prefer watching videos on a larger screen, you can use **Air-Play** to stream content from your iPhone to your Apple TV or other

AirPlay-compatible devices. To do this, open the video you want to watch, tap the **AirPlay** icon (a rectangle with an arrow), and select the device you want to stream to. This allows you to enjoy your favorite shows and movies on a bigger screen with better audio quality.

The **Picture-in-Picture** (PiP) feature lets you watch videos while using other apps. To enable PiP, start playing a video and then swipe up from the bottom of the screen (or press the home button) to return to the home screen. The video will reduce to a small, movable, and resizable window, enabling you to multitask without missing any action.

Chapter 9

Learning New Skills

Using the Tips App

The Tips app is a valuable resource for discovering new features, learning shortcuts, and getting the most out of your device. Represented by a yellow icon with a lightbulb, the Tips app offers practical advice and helpful tutorials tailored to enhance your iPhone experience.

To get started, open the **Tips** app from your home screen. Upon opening the app, you'll be greeted with a series of tips organized into categories such as **What's New in iOS**, **Get to Know iPhone**, and **Photos and Camera**. Each tip is designed to introduce you to different functionalities and features that can make using your iPhone more enjoyable and efficient.

For instance, in the **What's New in iOS** section, you might find tips on the latest updates and new features introduced in the current iOS version. These tips can help you stay updated and take advantage of new capabilities as soon as they become available. For example, you could learn about new privacy settings that give you more control over your data or discover enhancements in the Messages app that make communicating with friends and family more fun.

The **Get to Know iPhone** section is perfect for those who are new to the iPhone or want to familiarize themselves with its basic functions. Here, you might find tips on how to customize your home screen, use Siri for voice commands, or navigate using gestures. These tips provide step-by-step instructions that are easy to follow, helping you become more comfortable with your device.

In the **Photos and Camera** section, you'll find tips on how to take better photos, use different camera modes, and organize your photo library. For example, you might discover how to use Portrait mode to take professional-looking photos with a blurred background or learn how to create albums to keep your photos organized. These tips can help you make the most of your iPhone's powerful camera features and capture memories in the best possible way.

The Tips app also offers a **Search** function, allowing you to find specific tips by entering keywords. This is particularly useful if you're looking for help with a specific feature or want to learn more about a particular aspect of your iPhone. For example, if you're interested in learning how to use FaceTime, simply type "FaceTime" into the search bar, and the app will display relevant tips and tutorials.

To receive regular updates and notifications about new tips, you can enable notifications for the Tips app. Go to **Settings > Notifications > Tips** and toggle on **Allow Notifications**. This way, you'll get timely advice and information right on your lock screen or in the Notification Center, ensuring you never miss out on useful insights.

One of the great features of the Tips app is its ability to save your favorite tips for easy access later. If you find a tip particularly helpful, tap the **Save** button. You can then access all your saved tips by tapping the **Saved** tab at the bottom of the screen. This feature allows you to quickly refer back to tips that you find especially useful, without having to search for them again.

Exploring Educational Apps

Exploring educational apps can open up a world of learning opportunities, from mastering new languages to understanding complex scientific concepts. Imagine being able to learn a new skill, dive into a fascinating subject, or help your grandchildren with their homework—all from the convenience of your phone. Whether you're looking to expand your knowledge, support your hobbies, or engage in lifelong learning, the App Store offers a variety of educational apps that cater to all interests and age groups. These apps can transform your iPhone into a portable classroom, library, or study aid, providing valuable resources at your fingertips.

To start, open the **App Store** and tap on the **Search** tab. Enter keywords related to your interests, such as "language learning," "math," "history," or "science." You'll find a wide range of apps designed to educate and engage. Popular educational apps include **Duolingo** for language learning, **Khan Academy** for a broad range of subjects, and **TED** for inspirational talks and lectures.

For those interested in learning new languages, **Duolingo** is a highly recommended app. It offers courses in multiple languages, using fun and interactive methods to teach vocabulary, grammar, and pronunciation. The app tracks your progress and provides regular feedback, making it easy to stay motivated. You can set daily goals and practice at your own pace, whether you're a beginner or looking to brush up on your skills.

If you're passionate about history or science, the **Khan Academy** app provides comprehensive lessons on a wide range of topics. The app features video lectures, practice exercises, and quizzes that help reinforce your learning. For example, you can explore ancient civilizations, learn about significant historical events, or delve into biology and physics. The app's structured courses make it easy to follow along and track your progress.

For those who enjoy inspirational and educational talks, the **TED** app is a treasure trove of ideas and knowledge. You can watch TED Talks on various subjects, from technology and education to art and personal development. The app allows you to search for talks by topic, speaker, or popularity, providing endless opportunities to learn from experts and thought leaders around the world.

The **Coursera** app offers access to online courses from top universities and institutions. You can enroll in courses on a wide range of subjects, such as business, technology, health, and arts. Many courses offer certificates upon completion, which can be a fantastic way to enhance your skills and knowledge. The app allows you to watch video lectures, participate in discussions, and complete assignments at your own pace.

For a more interactive learning experience, **Quizlet** is an excellent app that uses flashcards and games to help you study. You can create your own flashcards or use sets created by other users. The app covers a wide range of subjects, making it a versatile tool for learning new concepts and preparing for exams. For example, you can use Quizlet to memorize historical dates, learn scientific terms, or practice foreign language vocabulary.

If you enjoy reading, the **Audible** app provides access to a vast library of audiobooks, including educational and self-improvement titles. Listening to audiobooks can be a convenient way to learn while multitasking, whether you're driving, exercising, or doing household chores. You can find books on virtually any topic, from biographies and memoirs to how-to guides and textbooks.

For younger learners, educational apps like **ABCmouse** and **PBS Kids** offer engaging content designed to teach foundational skills in reading, math, and science. These apps use games, videos, and interactive activities to make learning fun and engaging for children. They can be a great resource for grandparents who want to support their grandchildren's education in a playful and interactive way.

Staying Curious with Siri

Siri, Apple's intelligent virtual assistant, can be a powerful tool for satisfying your curiosity and simplifying your daily tasks on the iPhone 15. Whether you're seeking information, setting reminders, or managing your schedule, Siri is always ready to help with just a voice command. Imagine asking a question or giving a command and instantly receiving a response or having the task completed for you. This hands-free convenience can be especially helpful when your hands are full or when you need information quickly.

To activate Siri, you can either say "Hey Siri" followed by your command or press and hold the side button on your device. Siri can assist with a wide range of queries and tasks. For example, if you're curious about the weather, simply say, "Hey Siri, what's the weather like today?" Siri will provide a detailed weather forecast for your location, helping you plan your day accordingly.

Siri is also great for getting quick answers to factual questions. You might ask, "Hey Siri, who won the Nobel Prize in Literature in 2020?" or "Hey Siri, how many calories are in an apple?" Siri uses information from the web and other sources to provide accurate and timely answers, making it a handy tool for satisfying your curiosity about the world.

You can set reminders and alarms by saying, "Hey Siri, remind me to take my medication at 8 PM" or "Hey Siri, set an alarm for 6 AM." These voice commands ensure you stay on track with your daily tasks without needing to manually enter reminders or alarms into your iPhone.

Siri can also help you stay organized by managing your calendar. You can create and update events by saying, "Hey Siri, schedule a meeting with John tomorrow at 3 PM" or "Hey Siri, add a dentist appointment to my calendar for next Tuesday at 10 AM." This feature is especially helpful for tracking appointments and important dates, ensuring you never miss a key event.

For those moments when you want to learn something new, Siri can provide valuable information. You might ask, "Hey Siri, how do I make lasagna?" or "Hey Siri, tell me a fun fact about dolphins." Siri can search the web for recipes, facts, and other useful information, making it a great companion for expanding your knowledge and satisfying your curiosity.

If you enjoy listening to music or podcasts, Siri can help you find and play your favorite content. Simply say, "Hey Siri, play some jazz music" or "Hey Siri, play the latest episode of my favorite podcast." Siri integrates with Apple Music and Apple Podcasts to provide seamless playback of your chosen media, enhancing your listening experience.

Navigating your iPhone is more convenient with Siri's assistance. You can open apps, send messages, and make phone calls using voice commands. For instance, you can say, "Hey Siri, open the Photos app" or "Hey Siri, call Susan." These commands streamline your interactions with your iPhone, allowing you to perform tasks quickly and efficiently.

Siri's capabilities extend to controlling smart home devices if you have HomeKit-enabled accessories. You can control lights, thermostats, and other smart devices by saying, "Hey Siri, turn off the living room lights" or "Hey Siri, set the thermostat to 72 degrees." This integration makes managing your home environment easier and more convenient.

Chapter 10

Managing Your iPhone

Updating Your iPhone

Updating your iPhone with the latest software is crucial for optimal performance, accessing new features, and maintaining security. Apple regularly releases updates for iOS, the operating system that powers your iPhone, and these updates can include everything from bug fixes and performance improvements to exciting new functionalities. Imagine always having the latest tools and features at your disposal, enhancing your user experience and keeping your device secure.

To check for updates, go to **Settings > General > Software Update**. Your iPhone will automatically check for any available updates. If an update is available, you'll see a message indicating the updated version of iOS and a brief description of the changes it includes. Tap **Download and Install** to begin the update process. You may need to enter your passcode to confirm the installation.

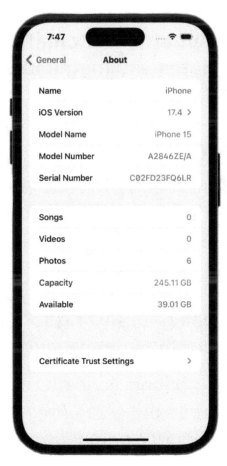

Before updating your iPhone, it's a good idea to back up your data to ensure that your information is safe in case anything goes wrong during the update. You can back up your iPhone using iCloud by going to **Settings > [your name] > iCloud > iCloud Backup** and tapping **Back Up Now**. Alternatively, you can use a computer to back up your device through iTunes or Finder, depending on your operating system.

During the update process, your iPhone will download the update file, verify it, and then install the new software. This process can take some time, so it's best to ensure your iPhone is connected to a reliable Wi-Fi network and has sufficient battery life or is plugged into a power source. Once the installation is complete, your iPhone will restart, and you'll be running the latest version of iOS.

Enabling automatic updates is a convenient way to ensure your iPhone stays up to date without you having to manually check for updates. To enable this feature, go to **Settings > General > Software Update > Automatic Updates** and toggle on **Download iOS Updates** and **Install iOS Updates**. With these settings enabled, your iPhone will automatically download and install updates overnight while connected to Wi-Fi and charging.

Keeping your apps updated is equally important, as app developers frequently release updates to add new features, improve performance, and fix bugs. To update your apps, open the **App Store** and tap on your profile picture in the top right corner. Scroll down to see a list of apps with available updates and tap **Update All** to install the latest versions. You can also enable automatic app updates by going to **Settings > App Store** and toggling on **App Updates** under the Automatic Downloads section.

Updating your device not only provides access to the latest features but also enhances your device's security. Apple incorporates security patches in many updates to protect against new threats and vulnerabilities. By keeping your iPhone and apps up to date, you ensure that your personal information and data remain secure.

Managing Storage

Efficiently managing the storage ensures that you have enough space for all your photos, apps, and files, while keeping your device running smoothly. With a few simple steps, you can easily monitor and optimize your storage, preventing the frustration of running out of space at crucial moments.

To check your storage usage, go to **Settings > General > iPhone Storage**. Here, you can view a breakdown of how much space each app and category of content is using. This overview helps you identify which apps or files are taking up the most space, allowing you to make informed decisions about what to keep and what to delete. For example, you might notice that photos and videos are consuming a large portion of your storage. Tapping on **Photos** provides further details and recommendations for freeing up space, such as enabling **iCloud Photos** to store your media in the cloud instead of on your device.

To manage your storage more effectively, consider offloading unused apps. This feature allows you to remove apps you rarely use while keeping their data intact, so you can easily reinstall them without losing any information. To enable this feature, go to **Settings > General > iPhone Storage** and tap **Enable** next to **Offload Unused Apps**. Your iPhone will automatically offload apps you haven't used in a while, freeing up space without affecting your app data.

Another useful strategy is to delete old messages and attachments. Over time, text messages, especially those with photos and videos, can accumulate and take up significant storage space. To set your iPhone to automatically delete old messages, go to **Settings**

> Messages > Keep Messages and select a shorter duration, such as 30 days or 1 year. This way, your device will automatically remove older messages and free up storage.

Clearing the cache and data from apps like Safari can also help reclaim storage space. To do this, go to **Settings > Safari** and tap **Clear History and Website Data**. This will remove your browsing history, cookies, and other data, freeing up space and potentially improving the performance of the Safari app.

Using cloud storage services like **iCloud Drive**, **Google Drive**, or **Dropbox** is another effective way to manage your iPhone's storage. These services allow you to store files, photos, and videos in the cloud, reducing the amount of local storage used on your device. To set up iCloud Drive, go to **Settings > [your name] > iCloud > iCloud Drive** and toggle it on. You can also download apps for Google Drive or Dropbox from the App Store and follow their respective setup instructions.

If you need more storage space, consider upgrading your iCloud storage plan. Apple offers several iCloud storage plans, starting with 5GB of free storage and extending to larger capacities for a monthly fee. To upgrade your iCloud storage, go to **Settings > [your name] > iCloud > Manage Storage > Change Storage Plan** and select the plan that best suits your needs.

Managing your photos is another key aspect of storage optimization. Using the **Optimize iPhone Storage** feature in iCloud Photos ensures that full-resolution photos and videos are stored in iCloud, while smaller, device-sized versions are kept on your iPhone. To enable this, go to **Settings > [your name] > iCloud > Photos** and select **Optimize iPhone Storage**. This feature helps you save space on your iPhone while still having access to your entire photo library.

Protecting Your iPhone

Protecting your iPhone is crucial to ensure the safety of your personal information and the longevity of your device. By following some essential steps, you can secure your iPhone against potential threats and keep it functioning optimally.

One of the first steps is setting up **Face ID** or **Touch ID**. These biometric authentication methods offer a secure and convenient way to unlock your device. To set up Face ID, go to **Settings > Face ID & Passcode**, and follow the instructions to scan your face. For Touch ID, go to **Settings > Touch ID & Passcode**, and follow the prompts to scan your fingerprint. These features not only help secure your iPhone but also make it easier to access your device and apps quickly.

Creating a strong passcode is another vital security measure. Instead of using simple codes like "1234" or "0000," opt for a more complex six-digit passcode. To change your passcode, go to **Settings > Face ID & Passcode** or **Settings > Touch ID & Passcode**, then tap **Change Passcode**. Follow the prompts to enter a new, stronger passcode.

Enabling **Find My iPhone** is essential for locating your device if it's lost or stolen. This feature lets you track your iPhone's location, play a sound to help find it, or remotely lock and erase it to secure your data. To enable Find My iPhone, go to **Settings > [your name] > Find My > Find My iPhone**, and toggle it on. Make sure **Send Last Location** is also enabled, so your iPhone's location is automatically sent to Apple when the battery is critically low.

Keeping software up to date is crucial for security. Software updates often include patches for vulnerabilities and improvements in security features. To ensure your iPhone stays up to date, go to **Settings > General > Software Update** and enable **Automat-**

ic Updates. This ensures your device will automatically install updates overnight while it's charging and connected to Wi-Fi.

Regularly backing up protects your data in case your device is lost, stolen, or damaged. You can back up your iPhone using **iCloud** or a computer. To back up with iCloud, go to **Settings > [your name] > iCloud > iCloud Backup** and toggle it on. Select **Back Up Now** to create a current backup. To back up using a computer, connect your iPhone to your computer and use **Finder** (on macOS Catalina or later) or **iTunes** (on earlier macOS versions or Windows) to back up your data.

Managing app permissions and settings enhances your privacy and security. Go to **Settings > Privacy** to review and adjust permissions for apps that access your location, contacts, photos, and other sensitive data. Limiting permissions to only what's necessary helps protect your personal information.

Using a secure Wi-Fi network is important when accessing the internet. Avoid public Wi-Fi networks that aren't password-protected, as they can expose your data to potential hackers. At home, make sure your Wi-Fi network is secured with a strong password and encryption, such as WPA3 or WPA2. You can set this up in your Wi-Fi router's settings.

Finally, consider using a sturdy case and screen protector to physically protect your iPhone. A good case can prevent damage from drops and bumps, while a screen protector can safeguard against scratches and cracks. These accessories help prolong the life of your device and keep it looking new.

Chapter 11

Customizing Your Experience

Personalizing Settings

Customizing your iPhone 15 to suit your preferences can enhance your overall experience and make your device feel uniquely yours. The iPhone offers a wide range of settings that you can adjust to personalize everything from the appearance of your home screen to the sounds your device makes.

To start personalizing your iPhone, go to **Settings**. One of the first things you might want to change is the **Wallpaper**. A visually appealing wallpaper can make your home screen more enjoyable to look at. To change your wallpaper, go to **Settings > Wallpaper > Choose a New Wallpaper**. You can select from Apple's gallery of dynamic, still, or live wallpapers, or choose a photo from your own library. Once you select an image, you can set it as your wallpaper for the lock screen, home screen, or both.

Adjusting the **Display & Brightness** settings can also enhance your viewing experience. Go to **Settings > Display & Brightness** to adjust the brightness level and enable **True Tone**, which automatically adjusts the display based on the ambient lighting conditions to make colors appear consistent. You can also enable **Dark Mode**, which changes the overall theme to a darker color scheme that's easier on the eyes in low-light conditions. To turn on Dark Mode, tap **Dark** under the Appearance section.

Personalizing your **Ringtones** and **Alert Tones** adds a touch of individuality to your device. Go to **Settings > Sounds & Haptics** to select different ringtones and alert tones for incoming calls, texts, and notifications. You can choose from the default sounds provided by Apple or purchase new tones from the **Tone Store**. Customizing these sounds helps you quickly identify incoming notifications and adds a personal touch to your device.

The **Control Center** offers quick access to frequently used controls and apps. To personalize the Control Center, go to **Settings > Control Center > Customize Controls**. Here, you can add, remove, and rearrange the controls to suit your needs. For example, you might add shortcuts for the flashlight, calculator, or screen recording, making it easier to access these features with a simple swipe.

Enabling and customizing **Do Not Disturb** can help you manage interruptions and focus on what matters. Go to **Settings > Do Not Disturb** to set up this feature. You can schedule Do Not Disturb to activate automatically during specific times, such as when you're sleeping or in a meeting. You can allow calls from specific contacts to come through even when Do Not Disturb is enabled, ensuring you don't miss important calls.

For accessibility and convenience, you might want to adjust the **Text Size** and **Display & Text Size** settings. Go to **Settings > Display & Brightness > Text Size** to adjust the size of the text on your iPhone. If you need more visibility options, go to **Settings > Accessibility > Display & Text Size** to enable features like Bold Text, Increase Contrast, and Reduce Transparency.

Widgets are another way to personalize your home screen. Widgets provide at-a-glance information and quick access to your favorite apps and features. To add widgets, press and hold on an empty space on your home screen until the apps start to jiggle, then tap the **+** button in the top left corner. Select the widget you want to add and choose a size. You can place widgets on your home screen or in the Today View for easy access.

Creating custom **Shortcuts** can streamline tasks and enhance your productivity. The **Shortcuts** app allows you to create automation for routine actions, such as sending a message when you leave home or starting a playlist when you arrive at the gym. Open the Shortcuts app and tap **Create Shortcut** to start building your custom automation.

Using Widgets

Widgets on your iPhone 15 provide quick access to information and essential functions directly from your home screen. They offer a glanceable view of important data, such as weather updates, calendar events, and news headlines, without having to open the corresponding apps. Customizing widgets can enhance your iPhone experience by keeping the information you need most readily available.

To start using widgets, press and hold an empty space on your home screen until the apps begin to jiggle. Tap the **+** button in the top left corner to open the

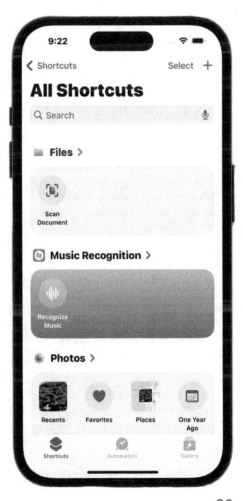

widget gallery. Here, you'll find a variety of widgets from both Apple and third-party apps. Browse through the selection or use the search bar to find specific widgets.

Once you find a widget you want to use, tap on it to view the available sizes. Widgets come in small, medium, and large sizes, each offering different amounts of information. Select **Add Widget** to include it on your Home Screen. You can then drag it to your desired location and position it among your app icons.

To customize the information displayed by a widget, press and hold the widget on your home screen until a menu appears, then tap **Edit Widget**. Depending on the widget, you can adjust settings such as the location for weather widgets or the calendar for upcoming events. Customizing widgets ensures that they display the most relevant information for you.

Smart Stacks are a special type of widget that can contain multiple widgets in one space. The iPhone intelligently rotates through the widgets in the stack based on your usage patterns, time of day, and location, showing the most relevant widget when you need it. To create a Smart Stack, add the Smart Stack widget from the gallery, or drag and drop widgets of the same size on top of each other to create your custom stack. You can edit the stack by pressing and holding it, then selecting **Edit Stack** to rearrange or remove widgets.

You can also place widgets in the **Today View**, which you access by swiping right on the home screen or lock screen. To add widgets to the Today View, scroll to the bottom of the Today View and tap **Edit**. Tap the **+** button next to the widgets you want to add, and they will appear in your Today View for easy access.

Some useful widgets to consider adding include:

- **Weather**: Provides real-time weather updates and forecasts.

84

- **Calendar**: Displays upcoming events and appointments.

- **Reminders**: Shows your tasks and to-do lists.

- **Photos**: Rotates through your favorite photos and memories.

- **News**: Keeps you updated with the latest headlines and stories.

- **Fitness**: Tracks your activity rings and workout summaries.

For those who like to stay organized, adding a **Notes** or **Reminders** widget can help keep your tasks and ideas front and center. The **Battery** widget is also helpful, as it shows the battery levels of your iPhone and connected devices like AirPods or Apple Watch.

Accessibility Customizations

Making your device more accessible ensures that it meets your individual needs, providing a user-friendly experience for everyone. Apple offers a range of accessibility settings designed to help those with vision, hearing, and motor impairments. These customizations can enhance your interaction with your device and make daily tasks easier.

One of the most versatile accessibility features is **AssistiveTouch**. This feature provides an on-screen menu that lets you perform actions typically done with physical buttons, such as taking screenshots, adjusting volume, and accessing the home screen. To enable AssistiveTouch, go to **Settings > Accessibility > Touch > AssistiveTouch** and toggle it on. You can customize the AssistiveTouch menu by adding or removing functions and adjusting the opacity of the on-screen button.

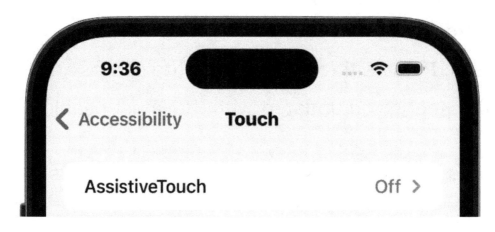

Customizing touch and motion settings can also make your iPhone more comfortable to use. For instance, **Touch Accommodations** helps if you have difficulty touching the screen accurately. To enable this, go to **Settings > Accessibility > Touch > Touch Accommodations** and adjust the settings to fit your needs. Options include Hold Duration, Ignore Repeat, and Tap Assistance, which help fine-tune how the screen responds to your touch.

For users with vision impairments, the iPhone offers several enhancements. **VoiceOver** is a screen reader that gives spoken descriptions of what's on your screen. To enable VoiceOver, go to **Settings > Accessibility > VoiceOver** and toggle it on. You can adjust the speaking rate and verbosity to suit your preferences. VoiceOver also supports gestures to navigate your iPhone, such as swiping and tapping.

The **Zoom** feature allows you to magnify the screen, making it easier to read small text or view details. To enable Zoom, go to **Settings > Accessibility > Zoom** and toggle it on. You can double-tap with three fingers to activate Zoom and use the same gesture to adjust the zoom level. Additionally, the **Magnifier** feature uses your camera as a digital magnifying glass. Enable it by going to **Settings > Accessibility > Magnifier**.

Adjusting **Display & Text Size** settings can also improve readability. Go to **Settings > Accessibility > Display & Text Size** to enable options like Bold Text, Larger Text, Increase Contrast, and Reduce Transparency. These settings can make the screen easier to read and navigate.

For those with hearing impairments, **Hearing Devices** allows you to connect compatible hearing aids and use them with your iPhone. Go to **Settings > Accessibility > Hearing Devices** to pair your hearing aids. **Live Listen** is another useful feature that uses your iPhone's microphone to amplify sound and send it directly to your hearing aids or AirPods. Enable it in **Settings > Control Center > Customize Controls** and add the Hearing control.

Sound Recognition notifies you of specific sounds such as doorbells, alarms, and baby cries. To enable this feature, go to **Settings > Accessibility > Sound Recognition** and toggle it on. Customize which sounds you want your iPhone to recognize by selecting them from the list.

For users with motor impairments, **Switch Control** allows you to use switches or other adaptive devices to control your iPhone. Set it up by going to **Settings > Accessibility > Switch Control**. Follow the prompts to configure your switches, allowing you to navigate and interact with your device without using the touchscreen.

Voice Control is another powerful tool that lets you operate your iPhone using only your voice. To set it up, go to **Settings > Accessibility > Voice Control** and follow the instructions to enable it. You can use voice commands to open apps, adjust settings, type text, and more, making it easier to use your iPhone hands-free.

Chapter 12

Troubleshooting Common Issues

Basic Troubleshooting Steps

Every now and then, you might encounter a hiccup with your device. Whether it's an app that suddenly stops responding, a battery that drains too quickly, or a Wi-Fi connection that just won't cooperate, these issues can be frustrating. But don't worry you're not alone, and many common problems have simple solutions. Understanding a few basic troubleshooting steps allows you to swiftly resolve these issues and return to enjoying your device.

One of the first steps in troubleshooting is to restart your iPhone. This simple action can resolve many minor issues and refresh the system. To restart your iPhone, press and hold the side button and either volume button until the power off slider appears. Slide to turn off your iPhone, wait a few seconds, and then hold down the side button until the Apple logo appears again.

If an app is unresponsive or behaving strangely, force quitting the app can help. Swipe up from the bottom of the screen and pause in the middle to open the app switcher. Find the problematic app and swipe it up and off the screen to close it. Then, reopen the app to see if the issue is resolved.

Clearing the cache and temporary data of apps can also help resolve performance issues. For Safari, go to **Settings > Safari** and tap **Clear History and Website Data**. This will remove browsing history, cookies, and other data, potentially improving performance. For other apps, you may need to delete and reinstall the app to clear its cache.

If your iPhone is running slowly or acting erratically, checking for software updates can be beneficial. Apple regularly releases updates that include bug fixes and performance enhancements. To check for updates, go to **Settings > General > Software Update**. If an update is available, follow the prompts to download and install it.

Resetting network settings can resolve connectivity issues with Wi-Fi, Bluetooth, or cellular networks. To reset network settings, navigate to **Settings > General > Reset > Reset Network Settings**. This will erase saved Wi-Fi passwords, Bluetooth connections, and VPN settings, so you'll need to reconfigure these after the reset.

If your iPhone's battery is draining quickly, checking battery usage can help identify the cause. Navigate to Settings > Battery to view a breakdown of battery usage by app. If an app is consuming an excessive amount of battery, consider updating, limiting its usage, or uninstalling it.

For issues related to sound, such as no audio during calls or when using certain apps, ensure that the **Do Not Disturb** feature is not enabled. Go to **Settings > Do Not Disturb** and make sure it is turned off. Also, check the **Mute** switch on the side of your iPhone to ensure it is not set to silent.

In cases where you're experiencing problems with your iPhone's display, such as unresponsive touch or incorrect colors, adjusting the display settings might help. Go to **Settings > Display & Bright-**

ness and adjust the brightness, True Tone, and Night Shift settings. If the issue persists, you may need to contact Apple Support for further assistance.

Performing a factory reset should be considered a last resort, as it will erase all data and settings on your iPhone. To perform a factory reset, go to **Settings > General > Reset > Erase All Content and Settings**. Make sure to back up your data before performing this step. After the reset, you can restore your data from an iCloud or iTunes backup.

Connectivity Issues

Experiencing connectivity issues with your iPhone can be frustrating, especially when you rely on your device for staying connected with loved ones, accessing important information, and enjoying online services. Whether it's a Wi-Fi connection that keeps dropping, Bluetooth that won't pair, or cellular data that isn't working, these problems can disrupt your daily routine. Understanding some basic troubleshooting steps can help you quickly resolve these connectivity issues and restore your connection.

If you're having trouble with your **Wi-Fi connection**, start by checking if other devices can connect to the same network. This can help determine if the issue is with your iPhone or the network itself. If other devices are working fine, try toggling the Wi-Fi on your iPhone off and back on. Go to **Settings > Wi-Fi** and switch the Wi-Fi off, wait a few seconds, then turn it back on. This simple step often resolves minor connectivity issues.

Restarting your router can also help. Disconnect the router, wait for about 30 seconds, and then reconnect it. Once the router has restarted, try reconnecting your iPhone to the Wi-Fi network. If the problem persists, forgetting the network and reconnecting can help. Go to **Settings > Wi-Fi**, tap the **i** icon next to your network, and select **Forget This Network**. Next, reconnect by selecting the network from the list and entering the password.

For **Bluetooth issues**, start by ensuring that Bluetooth is enabled on your iPhone. Go to **Settings > Bluetooth** and toggle it on if it's off. If Bluetooth is already on and you're having trouble connecting to a device, try toggling Bluetooth off and on. Sometimes, just restarting both your iPhone and the Bluetooth device can solve the problem.

If the issue continues, forget the Bluetooth device and attempt to reconnect. Go to **Settings > Bluetooth**, tap the **i** icon next to the device, and select **Forget This Device**. Then, put the Bluetooth device in pairing mode and reconnect by selecting it from the list of available devices.

Cellular data issues can be particularly disruptive, especially when you're on the go. If your cellular data isn't working, first check if Airplane Mode is enabled. Go to **Settings** or open the **Control Center** and make sure Airplane Mode is turned off. If it's off and you're still having issues, try toggling Cellular Data off and on. Go to **Settings > Cellular** and switch off Cellular Data, wait a few seconds, and turn it back on.

Restarting your iPhone can also help resolve cellular issues. Press and hold the side button and either volume button until the power off slider appears. Slide to power off your iPhone, wait a few seconds, and then press and hold the side button until the Apple logo appears.

Resetting your network settings is another effective solution for persistent connectivity issues. This action will erase all saved Wi-Fi networks, Bluetooth connections, and VPN settings, so you'll need to reconfigure them afterward. To reset network settings, navigate to Settings > General > Reset > Reset Network Settings. Enter your passcode if prompted and confirm the reset.

If none of these steps resolve your connectivity issues, contacting your internet service provider or visiting an Apple Store for further assistance might be necessary. Sometimes, hardware issues or problems with your network provider can cause connectivity problems that require professional support.

Getting Help

Even with the best troubleshooting efforts, there may be times when you need additional support for your iPhone 15. Knowing where to turn for help can make a significant difference in resolving issues quickly and effectively. Whether you need technical assistance, repairs, or just some guidance on using your device, Apple offers several resources to support you.

The first place to look for help is the **Apple Support** app, which you can find on your iPhone. Open the app to access a wealth of information and troubleshooting tips for common issues. The app provides step-by-step guides on various topics, such as setting up your device, managing settings, and troubleshooting problems. You can also find answers to frequently asked questions and explore articles on different features of your iPhone.

If you prefer speaking with a support representative, you can contact Apple Support directly from the app. Tap on the **Get Support** tab, select your issue, and choose the option to call or chat with a support agent. This allows you to get personalized assistance from an Apple expert who can help you resolve your problem.

For in-person assistance, visiting an **Apple Store** is an excellent option. Apple Stores offer the **Genius Bar**, where you can make an appointment to get hands-on support from a trained technician. To schedule an appointment, open the Apple Support app or go to the **Apple Support** website, select **Find Locations**, and choose a convenient store. Booking an appointment ensures that you receive dedicated time with a technician who can diagnose and fix your issue.

If your iPhone needs repairs, the Apple Store can handle most hardware issues, including screen replacements, battery replacements, and other repairs. If your iPhone is still under warranty or covered by AppleCare+, some repairs may be free or offered at a reduced cost. Make sure to verify your warranty status before going to the store.

Online resources, such as https://support.apple.com, provide extensive information and troubleshooting tips. The website offers an extensive library of articles, guides, and user manuals that cover a broad array of topics. You can find the information you need by searching for specific issues or browsing by category. The website also offers video tutorials that can help you understand and use various features of your iPhone.

The **Apple Community** is another valuable resource where you can ask questions and get answers from other Apple users. The community is made up of knowledgeable users who can provide insights and solutions based on their own experiences. To join the community, visit the **Apple Support Community** website, sign in with your Apple ID, and start participating in discussions.

Updating your iPhone to the latest iOS version can frequently fix software-related issues. Apple frequently releases updates that provide bug fixes, security patches, and performance enhancements. To check for updates, go to **Settings > General > Software Update** and install any available updates.

In cases where you've exhausted all other options, performing a factory reset can be a last resort. This will erase all data and settings on your iPhone, so it's essential to back up your data first. To perform a factory reset, go to **Settings > General > Reset > Erase All Content and Settings**. After the reset, you can restore your data from an iCloud or iTunes backup.

Conclusions

We have reached the end of our journey exploring the extraordinary features of the iPhone 15. By now, we are confident you will agree that this device is an exceptional tool for enhancing our lives. If this guide has helped make your initial use of the iPhone 15 easier and more enjoyable, we can proudly say that we have achieved our goal.

We remind you that if you wish to support our project and future publications, simply leave a review on Amazon using the QR code, as explained in the first pages of the book.

Additionally, through the following QR code, you can access your bonuses. These have been designed to make your experience with the iPhone 15 even more engaging and useful, and to bid you farewell at the conclusion of the journey we have taken together.

Index

A

B

C

D